I Can Hear Him!
Understanding the Light of Christ

Written and Illustrated by

Shelby Menet

ISBN-13: 979-8-218-07039-7

Published by MenetBooks

Cover design by Shelby Menet and Chelsea Jackson

Edited and Typeset by Chelsea Jackson, Jackson Writing and Editing, LLC

DEDICATION

Dedicated to Alayna, Mitch, and Kate in hopes that you may always *listen* and act on your promptings.

Did you know there is a light? The sun, moon, and stars are where it is. It's in the earth around me. I have it in me. This light is the **light of Christ**, and it's a gift from Heavenly Father. If I **listen**, the light of Christ can help me see, feel, and make good choices.

Doctrine and Covenants 88:7–12

Like today, the sun is shining. I can feel His warmth on my skin, and if I **listen**, I can hear Him in my heart, saying, "Enjoy my warmth!"

Corinthians 4:6

But I have bad days too. Some days the clouds can get sad and cry big raindrops.

On days like this, it can be difficult to feel His **light**. When this happens, I can get sad and cry too.

Or I can **listen**, and I hear His **light** guiding me, saying, "Look for rainbows."

Doctrine and Covenants 88:67

SOME DAYS, THE WIND CAN GET PUSHY,

AND BELIEVE ME, SHE CAN PUSH HARD!

When this happens, I can get mad and push back.

Or I can **listen**, and I hear Him through His **light**, calming me, saying, "Remember to fly your kite."

Ether 4:12

Some days the clouds can get down and gray. When this happens, I can get down and gray with them and forget about His *light*.

Or I can **listen**, and I feel His **light** uplifting me, saying, "Be patient. The sun will return. It always does."

Doctrine and Covenants 50:24

Some days the clouds and sky can turn pale with embarrassment, which causes everything to freeze and snowflakes to fall. When this happens, I can focus on the cold.

Or I can **listen**, and I can feel Him encircle me in His **light**, saying, "Admire the beauty of the snowflakes. Each one is different."

Doctrine and Covenants 88:50

Some days, the clouds get angry with lightning and the roar of thunder. When this happens, I can get frightened!

Or I can **listen**, and I hear His **light** speak peace to my mind, saying, "Find comfort in a friend."

John 1:9

EVERY NIGHT THE SUN LIES DOWN TO SLEEP AND PULLS
HIS DARK BLUE BLANKET OVER THE SKY.

WHEN THIS HAPPENS, I CAN GET SCARED.

Or I can **listen** and trust His **light** to shine on me, saying, "Count my stars that illuminate the night sky."

Doctrine and Covenants 6:21

AS I JOYFULLY LIE DOWN . . .

ALMA 28:14

And dream of the gift God has given me, I know I have a light, and if I listen, I can hear Him!

3 Nephi 18:24

About the author

Shelby Menet's biggest achievement is her three children, who often are her muses for her stories and illustrations. She has always had a dream of illustrating children's books. **I Can Hear Him!: Understanding the Light of Christ** is her first book.

Shelby graduated from Brigham Young University-Idaho with her bachelor of arts in 2014. She currently loves teaching fine arts for kindergarten through 12th grade.

LEAVE A REVIEW!

If you enjoyed this book,
please consider leaving
an honest REVIEW
on Amazon or Goodreads
and share it with your friends!

Thank you!

www.ingramcontent.com/pod-product-compliance
Lightning Source LLC
LaVergne TN
LVHW072055070426
835508LV00002B/111